LOUISE ARNER BOYD
Arctic Explorer

Notable Americans

LOUISE ARNER BOYD
Arctic Explorer

Durlynn Anema

MORGAN
REYNOLDS
Incorporated

Greensboro

LOUISE ARNER BOYD: ARCTIC EXPLORER

Photo Credits: Marin County Historical Society

Library of Congress Cataloging-in-Publication Data

Anema, Durlynn.
   Louise Arner Boyd, Arctic explorer / Durlynn Anema.
     p. cm. -- (Notable Americans)
   Includes bibliographical references (p.).
   Summary: A biography of the woman who gave up a wealthy and pampered life to
make extensive explorations in the Arctic regions.
   ISBN 1-883846-42-0 (lib. bdg.)
   1. Boyd, Louise Arner, 1887-1970--Juvenile literature. 2. Women
explorers--California--Biography--Juvenile literature. 3.
Explorers--California--Biography--Juvenile literature. 4. Arctic regions--Discovery and
exploration--Juvenile literature. [1. Boyd, Louise Arner, 1887-1970. 2. Explorers. 3.
Women--Biography. 4. Arctic regions--Discovery and exploration.] I. Title. II. Series.

G762.B6 A83 2000
910'.92--dc21
[B]

                                             99-059448

Printed in the United States of America
First Edition

Dedicated to all youth—may your dreams be fulfilled through perseverance and faith.

Acknowledgements

All books are written with the help of many people. Appreciation especially is given to Jocelyn Moss, Research Director, Marin County Historical Society; Jerry Kobril, Photo Curator, MCHS; Marjorie Fountain, a new friend and wonderful interviewee; and Laura Shoemaker, my editor at Morgan Reynolds. Thanks to students who have heard my presentations on Harriet Chalmers Adams and Louise Arner Boyd, and who have given me inspiration to write about heroines of the past. And to my grandchildren, thank you for giving me encouragement. Impossible dreams can be accomplished— just keep the faith.

Contents

Louise Arner Boyd

Chapter One

A Pampered Life

Louise Arner Boyd always had money. The heir to the equivalent of a few billion dollars by today's standards, she could have led a life of leisure. Instead she chose adventure—becoming the first woman to extensively explore Arctic regions. Louise never regretted her decision.

When Louise was born on September 16, 1887, the only daughter of John Franklin Boyd and Louise Arner Boyd, the family fortune was already secure from John's astute partnership in the Standard Mine in Bodie, California. Louise's family, including her brothers Seth and John, divided their time between San Rafael, California, and a huge horse ranch in the foothills east of San Francisco Bay. Louise and her brothers lived a storybook life riding their horses over the grassy hillsides, studying under tutors, and traveling abroad. "I was a tomboy," Louise later commented. "I rode horseback with my brothers. Often we would pack our saddlebags and ride all day through the hills."

Louise's father, John Boyd, had left his parents' farm in the eastern United States to travel west when he was fourteen years old. He worked a series of mining jobs and eventually became a mine manager. He met Dan and Seth Cook, who became his partners in 1876. The trio began searching for a productive investment.

John was known for his honesty. He was a man people trusted, an unusual attribute in an era of quick money and shady schemes. When a potential gold strike in Bodie occurred in 1877, John and his partners bought the Standard Mine for $67,500 cash. It was a smart decision. The partners made over six million dollars profit before selling the mine in 1882. John Boyd was never active in the mining business again. Instead, he entered the investment business.

Louise's mother was the niece of Dan and Seth Cook. She arrived in California in 1874, coming west with her grandfather and mother, who had tuberculosis. Her father had died after serving in the Civil War. Her uncles convinced her mother and grandfather that California's healthy climate might cure the tuberculosis.

In 1883, when John Franklin Boyd was forty and Louise Arner was twenty-one, the couple married and moved to Maple Lawn, their new San Rafael home built by Seth and Ira Cook. They commuted between this mansion and Oakwood Park Stock Farm, a ranch in the hills across San Francisco Bay.

From left to right: Louise, her mother, Seth, and John.

Louise and her brothers had servants for their every need. They had a Scottish governess to watch over them, and an Irish cook who prepared their meals. There were maids to clean, gardeners to prune rosebushes and trim grass, and stable boys to brush down the children's horses after long rides.

The governess tutored Louise and her brothers when they were young. Louise loved learning about new things and devoured books. She especially enjoyed history and geography, her strongest subjects in school. Years later she often said she was "a born geographer."

The three children regularly accompanied their parents to their San Francisco home. Louise loved these trips. She and her mother shopped for the newest styles and went for tea at the Palace Hotel. Her favorite outings were going to the theater and to the ballet. She was thrilled by the graceful movements of the ballerinas but never wanted to be a dancer. Later, she would become a patroness of the ballet and symphony.

As the only girl, Louise learned what was expected of young ladies during the Victorian era. Her mother carefully taught her to serve tea and entertain guests. She used these skills throughout her lifetime and enjoyed entertaining wherever she was. She also developed stylish habits of dress—Louise always wore a hat and gloves whenever she left the house. Her mother taught her a sense of style that would carry her from San Rafael to the British Court and beyond.

During the summers, the children roamed free at the Oakwood Park Stock Farm, swimming, shooting rifles, hiking, and wrestling. They often climbed Mt. Diablo in the East Bay and admired the view of the Pacific Ocean and Yosemite National Park.

At home in the evenings, the family enjoyed playing music and telling stories. Louise's mother played the piano, as did Louise; the boys played guitar. Louise's mother and father would tell their children stories from their childhoods in the East. Louise and her brothers became so fascinated by the tales of cold, snowy winters that sometimes the family would go to the docks to view the ships from Alaska. Louise read every book she could find about the North, and dreamed of the time when she could travel there.

On a morning in August 1901, disaster struck. Louise's seventeen-year-old brother, Seth, did not come down for breakfast. When his parents went to his room they found him dead of heart disease.

Eight months later they received a telegram from the Ventura County School in Southern California where sixteen-year-old John attended. He also had died—again from heart disease. Later, the family discovered both boys had been sick from rheumatic fever.

Maple Lawn turned into a place of sadness. Louise, at fourteen years old, became an only child and a constant companion to her parents. Her devastated father and mother never recovered from the deaths of their sons.

Louise's parents decided to remember Seth and John, Jr. with a living memorial. They donated the eastern portion of their estate to the city of San Rafael as a park. This was the same land where the children had played and rode horses. The Boyds also donated the gatehouse where the children played games on rainy days, which now houses the Marin County Historical Society.

Louise helped her parents arrange the dedication on April 29, 1905. The entire city of San Rafael shut down for the dedication and parade. In 1906, the Boyds donated a stained glass window at St. Paul's Episcopal Church in memory of Louise's brothers. Her parents sold Oakwood Park Stock Farm in 1906. That same year, Louise made her debut as a young lady of society.

After the deaths of her brothers, Louise elected to live a quiet life with her parents. They divided their time between Maple Lawn and San Francisco. Louise met a new group of friends when she enrolled at a private high school, but she knew when she graduated her plans for the future would be different from theirs. Her life revolved around her parents, and she often abandoned social activities to be with them. Louise was determined

The Boyd home, Maple Lawn, became gloomy after the deaths of Louise's brothers.

to continue to care for her parents as long as they needed her.

Although both of Louise's parents were often ill, they still found time and strength to travel. The family toured the United States and sailed to Europe. At one point they were entertained by President and Mrs. Theodore Roosevelt at the White House. During her travels, Louise finally saw her first snow, at age twenty.

To occupy herself on these trips, Louise decided to learn photography. With her typical determination she studied lenses, stops, and exposures. Seeing their daughter's new interest, Louise's parents hired a photography expert to help her.

Her brothers' deaths also meant that Louise would become heir to her father's investment business. Louise always had an interest in figures and details. At home and at her father's office, Louise and her father discussed business arrangements and investments. Louise attended company meetings with her father as he groomed her for her future role.

In 1909, at twenty-two-years old, she became president and manager of the Boyd Investment Company. She enjoyed this responsibility to make decisions that helped the fortune grow. She had a strong personality, enabling her to claim equal footing in the predominately male business world. Louise was not afraid to speak her mind.

Older men appreciated this young woman who had learned business and money management. Her strong personality, however, frightened possible suitors. Louise could not consider marriage anyway because of her devotion to her parents.

Although Louise was not considered a beautiful woman by the standards of the day, her appearance was so striking that people always noticed her when she entered a room. Her height and manner impressed everyone who met her. She held her head high, kept her shoulders back, and a smile was on her face whenever she met people. And of course, she dressed impeccably.

In 1919, her parents moved to a nursing home in San Francisco where Louise attended to their needs daily. Louise's mother died shortly after the move, and Louise's father followed a few months later in 1920. At thirty-two years old, Louise was completely alone with no relatives to share the fortune she had inherited.

Chapter Two

An Urge To Travel

Recovering from her parents' deaths was difficult for Louise. Louise had become so accustomed to waiting on her parents that her life now seemed empty. For the first half of 1920 she filled her time with activity. She decided to turn Maple Lawn into a place for parties and house guests.

Louise redecorated Maple Lawn because the house appeared so gloomy. Once the renovation was complete, she began to entertain friends, associates, community members, and visiting dignitaries. She became famous. for her parties, especially at Christmas. Members of the San Rafael police and fire departments were invited on Christmas Eve and her friends streamed through on Christmas Day.

Louise made friends easily because she was warm and caring. Many of her old friends from high school came to visit her. Louise became better acquainted with Janet

Coleman, who later accompanied her on several trips.

But by the end of 1920, Louise was bored with parties and entertaining. The thought of pouring tea and chairing fund raising events for the rest of her life wearied her. The passing of the Woman's Suffrage Act showed that attitudes toward women's roles had begun to change. Louise had plenty of experiences to mark her as an independent woman: Treading around the countryside with her brothers, presiding as president of the Boyd Investment Company, and traveling with her parents all over the world. She was accustomed to trying new things and hoped to discover something meaningful to do with her life. She was unsure, however, what that would be.

Louise decided traveling abroad might help her decide. From then on she never was without traveling companions. She easily found friends eager to take off and go wherever she wished. If they did not have enough money, Louise would pay for them.

Her first trip abroad was to France and Belgium. The widow of General Conger Pratt, an acquaintance of her parents, accompanied her. Never without a notebook, Louise busily recorded her impressions of the area, which was at the heart of World War I battles. In detail she described the ruined cities, bombed cathedrals, and devastated landscapes. Throughout the trip, she was deeply saddened by the devastation the war had caused.

During 1921, Louise traveled south from the Scandinavian countries to Spain, Portugal, and Italy, still recording the journey in her diary. She decided touring was more than simply viewing the usual tourist sights or attending parties. After both trips, she prepared a complete collection of her hundreds of photographs, labeling each one. "When I do anything, I like to do it thoroughly," she said.

Louise continued her study of photography back in the United States. At first she studied with experts from Northern California, but soon she realized she needed to expand her knowledge. She contacted Isaiah Bowman, Director of the American Geographical Society, and one of the foremost photographers and teachers in the world. He gladly accepted her as his pupil.

By 1924, Louise was bored with traveling to the usual destinations in Europe. She decided to go to Spitsbergen, Norway, a small archipelago lying in the Arctic Sea between the coasts of Norway and East Greenland. No tourist visited spots like this, which intrigued her. Later, she said she had chosen this unusual destination because of her fondness "of geography from earliest childhood." Exploration of the Arctic and polar regions also captivated the public in the 1920s.

Louise selected a small Norwegian tourist boat to visit Spitsbergen. As Louise stared at the stark blue pack ice

Louise Arner Boyd grew bored with the life of a debutante during the 1920s.

northwest of Spitsbergen, she became entranced by its color and vastness. She turned to the captain and said, "Some day I want to be way in there looking out, instead of looking in."

This "so-called uneventful trip" became the turning point of her life. She knew this first view of Arctic regions would not be her last. Louise finally had found her calling.

She returned home to plan her own Arctic expedition. Louise wrote to Francis DeGisbert, an expert on polar regions. She asked him to teach her everything he knew about the Arctic, and persuaded him to go on the trip. Later, she said he gave her the "best training."

Louise's plans came to a halt, however, in June 1925, when she was invited to England to be presented to King George V and Queen Mary at the Court of St. James. Louise was honored by this prestigious invitation, one desired by socialites throughout the world. The presentation demanded strict protocol. Almost everything she wore was dictated by rules of dress. Her gown was made of silver tissue and lavishly embroidered with pearls and rhinestones. Her court train was made of blue velvet, lined with blue tissue, and edged with chinchilla.

Along with 1000 others, Louise Arner Boyd was presented on June 29, 1925. The Lord Chamberlain announced each presentee to the king and queen. Later Louise attended a Garden Party at Buckingham Palace and visited Ascot Races.

The event, reported in all the English newspapers, quickly spread to American newspapers. The news in the eastern press then rapidly traveled west to San Francisco. Readers were impressed that an American woman and also a Californian had been presented at court.

Once the presentation ended, Louise returned to planning her trip. With her vast fortune, she could afford to perfect each detail. She wanted nothing to be amiss. For two years she organized her first Arctic journey.

The most important detail was chartering a good ship. She returned to Norway to hire an icebreaker, the *Hobby*. This ship was used to carry supplies by explorers Roald Amundsen and Admiral Richard Evelyn Byrd in their separate flights to the North Pole in 1926. Louise hired a fourteen-man Norwegian crew. To join her, Louise invited her old friend Janet Coleman; her polar teacher Francis DeGisbert; and Count and Countess Ignacio Rivadavia, close friends of the King of Spain, whom she had met while traveling abroad.

Louise planned to hunt and take photographs on her trip. Fascinated with the blue ice, tall icebergs, and glaciers, she wanted to capture their beauty with her camera. She also planned to hunt polar bears and seals— a respectable occupation during the 1920s.

The ship sailed into a land of deep blue water, ice, and snow. Louise photographed continuously. She shot glaciers at several different angles and topography during all times of the day. She also photographed the animals that inhabited the land and sea—polar bears, walruses, seals, and several species of Arctic birds.

As a favor, Louise collected botanical specimens whenever they landed. Her friend Alice Eastwood, the botanical curator of the California Academy of Sciences, encouraged her in this new hobby. In her youth, Louise had often collected flowers and plants while roaming the California hillsides. When she returned the Arctic specimens to Alice, she was delighted to learn she had found several new species on Northbrook Island which had not been reported previously.

During the voyage, Louise wore the same outfit she had used for hiking and riding trips through California, adding only an extra sweater and fur cap. She left her expensive fur coats at home because fur absorbs moisture. She did not need snowshoes because the snow was firm. Instead, she wore her old hiking boots. Comfort, not glamor, was Louise's main concern.

As they sailed within the Arctic Circle, Louise, her passengers, and the crew were the only people in the region. When she set foot on Franz Josef Land in Greenland, Louise became the first woman to do so. Yet, being recognized with firsts was not the purpose of her trip. The urge to find new places to explore had awoken in Louise—a desire to see things others had never seen. She wanted to be more than a tourist, she wanted to be an explorer.

During the six-week trip, Louise and her friends encountered no dangers. She told the captain she found the trip easier and more comfortable than she imagined it would be, which surprised him. He said the weather was worse than it had been in years.

Louise had become entranced with the beauty of the Arctic:

> ...isolation combined with danger made this beauty inaccessible and known to so few. I understood for the first time what an old seaman meant when he told me that once you had been in the Arctic and in the ice, you never could forget it, and always wanted to go back.

Newspapers around the world reported the trek. A London headline blazed "Girl Who Tamed the Arctic Wilds." One article even came up with this limerick:

> There was a young lady named Boyd
> Whom polar bears tried to avoid
> For when she fired shot
> They went where 'twas hot
> With a joy not unalloyed.

Although Louise had success hunting, it was the scenery that fascinated her. She vowed to return—but next time solely as an explorer of the Arctic.

Chapter Three

The Search for Amundsen

When Louise chartered the *Hobby* again in 1928, she had a new purpose—a scientific one. Once more she carefully planned every detail, from provisions to charting the journey's course. She hired three scientists to map the region, find botany samples, and determine ocean depths. Then she invited three friends to join her in exploring the northern and northeastern regions of Greenland.

Eagerly, Louise, her friends, and the scientists traveled to Tromsoe, Norway, to begin their journey. But when they arrived, momentous and tragic news greeted them. An Italian explorer, General Umberto Nobile, and his crew had crashed their dirigible, or hot air balloon, somewhere in the Arctic. The *Hobby* had just returned from a failed rescue search. Roald Amundsen, the famous Arctic and Antarctic explorer, had already set out in a plane to search for the lost men. Now he and his crew were also missing.

As these events swirled around her, Louise decided upon her course of action. She announced that the *Hobby* would be used by the Norwegian government for the search, and she would forgo her planned expedition. "How could I go on a pleasure trip when those twenty-two lives were at stake?" she asked.

Because she had chartered the *Hobby* and would be paying the expenses of the search mission, Louise and her friends became part of the rescue effort. There was never a doubt in her mind if she was doing the right thing. The *Hobby* was especially suited for the rescue because it was one of the few ships equipped to carry planes. Although the mission was under the direction of the Norwegian Navy, Louise insisted upon also flying the American flag.

The Norwegians were proud of their native son Roald Amundsen. He had entered the Norwegian Navy in 1893 and by 1897 was part of a team that traveled to the South Pole. In 1901 he began oceanographic research off the northeast coast of Greenland. Two years later he announced plans to relocate the position of the magnetic North Pole. During this trip he became the first person to take a ship from the Atlantic to the Pacific Ocean through the Northwest Passage. In 1911 he became the first man to reach the South Pole. In 1926 he flew over the North Pole under the command of General Umberto Nobile.

Louise was never afraid to perform the exacting tasks

of the crew. She spent many hours standing watch on the deck, searching for signs of encampments, a plane, or a boat in the distance. Later she said,

> Ice does such eerie things. There are illusions like mirages and there were times when we could clearly see tents. Then we'd lower boats and go off to investigate. But it always turned out the same—strange formations of the ice, nothing more.

During this voyage Louise also discovered what a "green" explorer she was. She did not know that the big sticks of what she called "candy" under her bunk actually were dynamite. The crew would use the dynamite to dislodge the ship if it were caught in the ice. When a fire broke out, Louise was appalled to discover there were no fire extinguishers aboard the ship, and the fire hose was caked with ice and useless. She was so frightened that on her next expedition she made it her personal responsibility to be sure ample fire extinguishers were aboard.

Back and forth across the Arctic waters the rescuers traversed for three months and ten thousand miles. They ventured many times along the west coast of Spitsbergen, as well as westward to the Greenland Sea and eastward to Franz Josef Land and into the pack ice. Not only was Louise making news in her frantic search, but she ended up going further north than on her previous trips. She wrote: "We returned here [Kings' Bay, Spitsbergen] after a week up north in the ice off the northwest part of Spitsbergen, but way north of 80 degrees 40 minutes, which breaks my former record for points north." (Louise had traveled to 81 degrees 13 minutes on her first trip.)

By this time Nobile and his crew had been found and rescued, but Amundsen still had not been recovered. Louise was determined to search as long as possible, although by mid-September bad weather often delayed the expedition. For days the *Hobby* encountered such violent storms that the planes were almost torn from the decks. Still Louise insisted on continuing until the ice packs and the oncoming Arctic winter prevented any further travel, and she realized it was impossible to persist. A longer stay could be very dangerous. She and the crew returned to Tromsoe, Norway, on September 22, almost three months after they had begun to search.

The futility of their search upset Louise. But she took pride that her expedition had been a recognized unit of the Norwegian Amundsen Rescue Expedition. When she returned to Norway, Louise learned she was to receive the Chevalier cross of a Knight of St. Olaf from King Haakon of Norway.

Her search effort gained headlines all over the world, including one in the local San Rafael newspaper in an article titled: "Arctic Search Fun for Marin 'Tomboy.' "

> Folks here think of her as the little tomboy school
> girl who rode her father's horses and frolicked
> with her two brothers...[but]...city residents are
> not surprised at her latest adventure. It puts the
> climax on some years of adventuring....She has
> spent years exploring the far places of earth and
> every once in a while comes home to say howdy
> and good-bye.

When she heard about her award presentation, Louise realized she did not have the appropriate clothing for the event. Her trunks contained only the rough clothes she had worn in the Arctic. Louise sailed to Paris on the first steamer she could find, and returned with a new fur coat and several gowns.

The royal carriage arrived promptly at her hotel to take her to the castle. First she received her Order of St. Olaf from the king, then had lunch with the royal family. She was the first American woman to receive the order and the third woman in the world to be honored. The French government also presented her with the Chevalier of the Legion of Honor, and other Scandinavian governments honored her for her rescue work, too.

Louise's 1928 trip brought her more than honors in the

midst of tragedy. During and after the voyage, Louise met several Arctic explorers. She chatted with them during breaks in the search effort and realized the immense area still waiting to be explored.

Among the men she met was Captain Eliaseen, who had been searching for the bodies of three balloonists lost in 1899. When, in 1930, Eliaseen found the frozen bodies, Louise attended the memorial service. Another influential explorer she met was Lauge Koch, a leading Danish scientist. He later would name a piece of Greenland after Louise following her 1931 expedition.

Louise also put her photography skills to good advantage during the voyage. She took several thousand photographs and almost 20,000 feet of motion picture film that detailed the search. She later donated these, along with extensive maps, to the American Geographical Society. The explorers she met repeatedly told her a competent photographer was necessary for proper mapping of this region.

Those words were all she needed to hear. She had the time and money to equip future exploration for scientific knowledge.

Chapter Four

The First Arctic Expedition

Now that her trips to the north served a definite purpose—contributing to the world's knowledge—Louise enjoyed her new expeditions to the Arctic far more than before. As official photographer for the 1928 expedition and the ones to follow, she took picture after picture. These photos would change how scientists looked at the coast of Greenland.

Louise no longer was a novice in polar seas. She understood navigation and the appearance and behavior of different forms of marine ice. As she became more familiar with the Arctic, the challenge of approaching land barred by wide belts of ice excited Louise. If her next expedition could cross this ice, she would gain access to new lands.

In 1931, Louise planned to visit the fiords of Franz Josef and King Oscar on the East Greenland coast. This trip would be a preliminary survey for a comprehensive expedition in 1933. She understood the need for small excursions to explore the extensive fiord area of East Greenland.

Louise hired the *Veslekari*. Its captain, Johan Olsen, was widely recognized for his seamanship. Built in 1918, the ship was 125 feet long and 27 feet wide, and strong enough to plow through wide belts of ice. It carried six additional boats—one motor dory, one motor launch, two large rowboats, and two American canoes—that could easily transport Louise and her passengers to the shore.

The scientists were bunked in six double cabins below deck. Louise, her maid, and her secretary housed themselves in two cabins on deck. In a third cabin, Louise stored her cameras, film, scientific equipment, and a dark room. The crew was quartered in the bow.

The ship also contained a library, dining salon, radio room, the captain's quarters, chart room, and bridge. It was a compact vessel, able to withstand the intensely cold weather of the Arctic North. The hold was completely filled with coal, barrels of fuel oil, nine tons of drinking water, and of course, dynamite to break up the ice packs.

Living conditions on the *Veslekari* were less than ideal. There was no running water. Louise, the crew, and the other scientists could not take a bath or shower. One had to wash off quickly to conserve water. Instead of fresh vegetables and meat, canned food lined the galley shelves. The ship was stocked with extra rations in case the explorers were stranded or stuck in ice.

Louise and the others wore heavy coats and hip boots to protect themselves from the big swells that washed over the sides of the ship. When she hiked on shore, Louise wore ski breeches and ski boots because they were not as heavy as field boots. She also wore sweaters instead of flannel shirts because they were easier to take off or put on when the temperature changed. When the weather became extremely cold, Louise donned extra wool underwear and another pair of socks.

During this trip, the expedition visited every fiord and sound in the region of Franz Josef and King Oscar Fiords. They also embarked on numerous shore trips. Louise took several thousand photographs illustrating the glaciers, sea ice, fine scenery, animal life, and flora. Louise also discovered a route between Kjerulf and Dickson Fiords that had never before been attempted. Her photos of the area were so good that Walter A. Wood, a surveyor from the New York Geographic Society, was able to map the region to scale without field measurements. The American Geographical Society constructed a large-scale topographic map from the same photographs.

Louise's education from Isaiah Bowman proved worthwhile. He not only taught her photography but introduced her to photogrammetry as well. Photogrammetry uses both photography and surveying to create reconnaissance-scale maps. When Bowman allowed Louise to become his pupil, photographers and geographers throughout the United States had been impressed; he had no patience before for women. They soon understood why Bowman had accepted her. Louise's passion for detail and hard work impressed everyone who saw her final photographs.

The expedition visited an Eskimo settlement at Scoresbysund. In the evening, they anchored in Rosevinge Bay. The main settlement and two other smaller ones formed the northernmost colony on the east coast of Greenland.

Everyone on the ship piled into the motor launch and headed for shore. The resident Danes and Eskimos were thrilled to have visitors. They came out to meet Louise and her shipmates in a launch and kayaks. The Eskimos paddled the kayaks swiftly, often turning over and over to demonstrate their skill.

The small town dotted the south slope of a hill: the administrator's house, a church, the pastor's house, a store, and work sheds. The operator of a seismographic and wireless station occupied a house with his wife where the visitors could stay. The Eskimos lived in houses made partly of wood and partly of turf with glass windows.

The Eskimo men danced, chanted, and sang for the group. Louise enjoyed their passionate dancing to the beat of tin pan drums. The men wore soft, knee-high seal

The residents of Scoresbysund lived in the northernmost settlement on East Greenland.

skin boots. The women wore boots similar to the men's, only more elaborate with fur and embroidery. Both men and women wore trousers wrapped with colorful silk at the waist, jewelry, beaded collars, and parkas. Their clothes were all decorated with artistic hand embroidery. They wore their hair pulled back tightly from their faces and high on the tops of their heads. Louise and her companions admired these Greenlanders for their quiet, charming manners, direct eyes, and faces radiating kindness.

Farther up the sound, the group visited other Eskimo settlements. These Eskimos returned on the *Veslekari* to attend the Lutheran church service at Scoresbysund. The church was wooden and painted dark red; its window sills were decorated a startling white. Over the entrance a large clock ticked the hours away, and above it, hung a bronze bell. On the morning of Sunday, August 16, eleven members of Louise's party and twenty-seven Eskimos attended the service together. The men sat on the left; the women on the right. The reverend spoke entirely in Greenlandic, except for a smattering of Danish for the visitors' benefit.

Later in the day, the Eskimos traveled on the *Veslekari* back to their homes. By this time, a bitter wind blew eastward off the inland ice cap. Louise watched with amusement as the Eskimos huddled in the engine room to keep warm.

Louise took this photograph of an Eskimo she visited on her 1931 journey.

She wrote in her journal that she and her companions

> were sad to see these splendid, kindly people leave the ship shortly after three o'clock in the morning. The women and children went ashore in the launch and the men in their kayaks raced each other to land, black silhouettes against the first rays of dawn.

As the ship departed, seven flashes appeared in a row in the sky, swiftly followed by as many rifle shots. The captain blew the *Veslekari*'s whistle to acknowledge the salute. Seven more flashes and another round of shots rang in farewell from the little group on shore.

The heavy pack ice along the coast prevented the ship from moving into several fiords. After two attempts, however, the ship did attain the inner reaches of Ice Fiord. To the best of Louise's knowledge, this region had never been visited. She described her findings in detail, noting that current topography maps might not be accurate. Her photographs later proved this to be true.

Inside Ice Fiord, Louise discovered the De Geer Glacier. Prior to this, only one glacier, the Jaette, had been known to end in Ice Fiord. Because the *Veslekari* had entered the fiord from the north, Louise was able to see this previously unknown glacier.

The expedition strengthened Louise's desire to continue Arctic research.

> It aroused in me a desire not only to continue until I had seen all of the region that is ordinarily accessible by ship...to record it with the camera as well and as thoroughly as possible...also to do what I could to add to the knowledge of features and conditions...for scientific investigation.

To acknowledge her impressive discovery, the Danish government named the area "Miss Boyd Land," or in Danish, *Weisboydlund*. Miss Boyd Land, located in Ice Fiord, includes the land lying between the De Geer Glacier and the Jaette Glacier.

Louise knew nothing about this honor until 1932. She received a letter from Dr. Lauge Koch that contained a published map with the new designation, Louise Glacier, at the head of Ice Fiord. The glacier is fed by the ice fields of Miss Boyd Land.

Chapter Five

Scientific Recognition

By 1933, Louise was forty-six years old and ready for the biggest Arctic expedition of her career to date. Sponsored by the American Geographic Society, this purely scientific enterprise would be well-organized, well-staffed, and well-equipped. Louise's two main purposes were to study glacial features and to record undersea soundings along the east coast of Greenland. As in 1931, Franz Josef and King Oscar Fiords became her main destinations.

Reporters now designated Louise as "the ice woman." The nickname referred both to her explorations and her demeanor. While appearing quiet and reserved, Louise was accustomed to commanding those around her. Her authoratative voice left no one in doubt of her abilities. She had become a tall, graceful woman with slightly graying hair, who no one failed to notice as she entered a room.

She began planning for the 1933 voyage soon after

returning from the 1931 preliminary expedition. This time she would venture beyond the belts of ice and deep into interior regions not yet visited by other explorers. She told reporters her goals:

> We shall do as much as we can in the time at our disposal, and I hope it will prove of some value to science. No doubt we shall have our troubles with the ice, but I know and understand the North, and we shall be back all right at the end of September.

The American Geographical Society helped Louise gather a prestigious group of scientists for the new expedition. Professor J. Harlen Bretz worked at the Geography Department of the University of Chicago and was named the trip's physiographer. O. M. Miller from the New York Geographical Society would act as surveyor, and William B. Drew of the Gray Herbarium at Harvard University was hired as botanist. However, Drew developed appendicitis a quarter of the way through the trip and had to be sent back. Louise took over this role, collecting over eighty specimens. Also among the scientists was Walter A. Wood of the New York Geographic Society as assistant surveyor. Wood had used Louise's photographs from 1931 to map East Greenland around Franz Josef and King Oscar Fiords. N. E. Odell, a Cambridge University geologist, joined the group with his wife. Louise was responsible for all the photographic work.

Because Louise was financing this expedition, she made all final decisions. She was well aware of her responsibility to get the expedition through all perils. "A slight error of judgment may mean another ship trapped in the closing ice," she later wrote.

Louise could not let go of all luxuries, and the meals on board the *Veslekari* in 1933 proved that she was accustomed to finery. Louise arranged to serve formal dinners in the dining salon that included delicacies from all over the world. Later, the scientists would comment that it was like being on a first-class steamer. Some of the scientists had never known this kind of luxury.

Not all of the scientists repaid Louise's kindness. Accustomed to orders by men, some did not respond to Louise respectfully. Louise simply ignored any tensions during the expedition—but these men were not invited on another trip.

One purpose of the voyage was to record undersea soundings. The *Veslekari* was fitted with an echo sounder—a new apparatus that could accurately record the contours of the ocean floor.

They would also chart the northeast coast of Greenland. The scientists planned to study the glacial features in the King Oscar Fiord and Franz Josef Fiord region. They

In 1931, the Danish government named this glacier for "the ice woman," Louise Arner Boyd.

would investigate and map small, critical areas to obtain an idea of typical physiographic features.

The expedition sailed from Alesund, Norway, on June 28, traveling northward 550 miles along the Norwegian coast. The scientists first tested the sonic depth finder, and discovered it could go down to 2200 meters (1200 fathoms). As the instrument moved along the ocean floor, Louise said they felt "as if we were in a ship with a glass bottom as we watched the instrument tracing the profile of the continental shelf and slope."

On July 4, the ship left the coast of Norway and headed westward into the open sea. This was Louise's third Fourth of July in the Arctic. She and her companions celebrated by flying the American flag and having a sumptuous meal that included caviar—or as sumptuous as was possible above a rolling sea. Water poured into the galley, making cooking and eating an "acrobatic feat."

The ship sailed towards its first destination, Jan Mayen Island, that lies midway between Norway and the east coast of Greenland. The majority of the time the island is cloaked in fog and heavy clouds. But on July 8, Louise and her crew saw a clear sky and Mt. Beerenberg, an extinct 7500 foot volcano.

The group took the motor dory ashore. They carried the mail Louise had volunteered to take to the Norwegian government's meteorological station. This was the first mail brought in almost eleven months. The men heard news on a radio but otherwise waited for ships like Louise's to bring newspapers, magazines, and cards and letters from loved ones. The men treated the entire party to cakes and tea, thrilled to have visitors. The explorers spent the day visiting with the meteorological team and walking along the coast.

When they left, the difficult portion of the expedition began. They had to cross the pack ice to get to the main Greenland coast. Captain Olsen was uncertain how long it would take because the width of the pack ice varies from year to year. In normal years it stretches from 100 to 150 miles, a journey that lasts ten days to two weeks or more.

When the *Veslekari* arrived at the pack, Louise and Captain Olsen were pleased to find the sea quite open. They were able to sail though in nineteen-and-a-half-hours. During the trip, the explorers spotted several polar bears and seals, which they had not seen in 1931. The Greenland coast was ice-free, with open water extending several miles to sea.

Now the party began to accomplish its main purpose: to explore extensively the fiord region of East Greenland by inlets that ran back as far as 120 miles. First they made soundings along the coast. As the crew worked, a seaplane landed. Dr. Lauge Koch informed them that the fiords were solidly closed by heavy ice, making entrance impossible. Louise was not discouraged; she knew enough about the region to have patience. She decided to sail along the coast and visit the hills by foot while they waited for the pack ice to break.

As she explored the land, Louise quickly discovered why it was named Myggbukta, and why the Eskimos left the region: The name means "Mosquito Bay." While taking photographs of the Eskimo ruins, Louise placed her camera on a tripod. Although she knew her lens worked correctly, she was unable to obtain a clear focus. Louise quickly realized the camera was not at fault. Mosquitoes covered the lens. Only by beating them off could Louise photograph her objective.

One night as Louise wrote some notes at a rough table in her cabin, a squall came up. The ship began to bounce "like an eggshell in a bathtub." Her oil lamp overturned, and the entire floor of her cabin caught fire. Quickly, she shut the door and ran for fire extinguishers and help. "I've confined the fire to my room," Louise told Captain Olsen. He yelled and rushed to her room with a fire extinguisher. Fortunately, the fire had not yet spread to the box beneath Louise's bunk that contained the emergency dynamite.

By July 22, ice conditions had changed and the ship was able to enter Franz Josef Fiord. Icebergs raised cleanly out of the blue water. The sky was clear. Louise thought the sight was breathtaking as she and the crew

The steamship *Veslekari* bore Louise safely on her 1931, 1933, 1937, and 1938 expeditions.

gazed from glaciers to snowcapped mountains. Slowly, they journeyed up the narrowing fiord. Louise described the view: "...canyon-like walls increased in high, vividness of color and beauty of form as one penetrates farther into its recesses."

Ice Fiord was well named. They encountered huge icebergs intermingled with so many smaller bergs they could not reach the fiord head. The captain chose another route, and encountering no difficulty, the ship gained the fiord's inner end. Louise and the scientists went ashore and set up camp at the lower end of Louise Glacier, 1600 feet above sea level. From there they hiked and explored.

As the ship sailed further, Louise was not prepared for the majestic beauty at the inner end of Franz Josef Fiord. Some of the highest mountains in that part of Greenland grace this area. The waterway narrowed. "It seems as if one were floating on the floor of an immense canyon," she described in her notebook. Louise and the scientists performed the majority of their work at this inlet.

One party traveled north to explore, and Louise and Captain Olsen went south. As they returned to the motor dory, Louise glimpsed another beautiful view and sent one of the crew for a camera. At the water's edge, he found a bottle with a note inside. The note was written in 1899 by a man searching for some lost balloonists.

These were the same balloonists she had heard about

In the name of science, Louise avidly photographed the flora, fauna, and topography she encountered on her expeditions.

in 1928 when she met Captain Eliaseen. She shivered in remembrance of the times her path had already crossed with them. She had attended their funeral in 1930 after Eliaseen had recovered their frozen bodies. In 1932, she was given the Andree Plaque, which was named for one of the balloonists, by the Swedish Anthropological and Geographical Society. These men had found out that the Arctic could be unforgiving, even to those who loved it.

During the next two weeks, the expedition camped inland, photographing, surveying, and taking soundings. Louise hiked over much of the region, taking pictures as she went. She was never afraid to hike where the men went and often walked ahead of them. Her strength amazed her male companions. Yet, she also remained feminine, powdering her nose before she ventured out on deck in the morning.

Never sea sick, Louise also never became ill on any of her trips. She said:

> Everyone who has gone on any expedition of mine has returned in better health than when he started....But I am careful to inquire into the health of every member of the party. One can't afford to have a sick person so far from a doctor or hospital.

Wind and sand were Louise's enemies. The sand was so fine in the valleys that it permeated everything, including her photographic equipment. Regardless of all possible care, the lenses and cameras often fell victims to the fine, gritty sand. Once, even though the tripod was well braced with stones, the wind hurled her large camera down a bank near the Mystery Lakes.

On August 23, the group finished their work and readied to leave. It was none too soon. A chill was always in the air and the nights were cold. Louise noted that while it was sunny, the weather was noticeably cooler than in 1931. Fog set in, so thick it took them two days of waiting aboard before they could move. On August 30 as they sailed, the day was sunless, raw and cold, and a high fog obliterated their view of all mountain summits.

Then, on September 1, the fog lifted. Early in the morning, Louise and the surveyors went by motor dory to land. The autumn colors were glorious; the vegetation very dry. They were thankful for a last clear view of Franz Josef Fiord but knew their departure was imperative. At ten in the morning they started eastward. Twelve hours later, they weighed anchor in a bay. Snow was falling within a few hundred feet of shore.

Two days later, the ship moved slowly at no more than a few knots. Then tragedy struck. The *Veslekari* hit ground at half past ten on the morning of September 3.

Quickly, Captain Olsen reversed the engines. At high tide, the ship had stuck and settled. Louise and Captain Olsen knew that all the other ships had left the east coast of Greenland, and they must rely on their own ingenuity to get afloat.

As the tide again went out, the ship settled a little more. The captain ordered the removal of some cargo. Thirty tons of seawater ballast, two motor boats, one rowboat, three and a half tons of fuel oil, and seventeen barrels of petrol were placed overboard. He hoped that between the lighter cargo and incoming tide the ship might become free. But the tide came and went—leaving them fast. They removed the coal. The ship had been lightened to fifty-four and a half tons. It seemed there was nothing else they could do.

Captain Olsen spotted an iceberg about 720 feet away. He ordered a cable lassoed around it and connected with the ship's winch. The motor dory shoved the berg as the winch pulled on the cable. The iceberg was grounded aft of the ship. They waited for the next tide.

With high tide and the engines full speed astern, Captain Olsen made another attempt. The winch pulled on the cable connected to the iceberg. The engines roared. The *Veslekari* came afloat once more—undamaged. Relieved, Louise later said, "Here was a case when an iceberg was a friend!"

They anchored and reloaded their petrol barrels and boats. They had enough coal left for the homeward journey, and began by half past twelve in the afternoon. Louise gave full credit to the seamanship of Captain Olsen and his crew for saving them. If they had not become free, they would have been stuck in the swiftly arriving ice all winter.

Their return to Norway was slow. High winds and rough seas forced them to stop several times. In July, the past winter's ice had been floating on the water. Now the coming winter's ice rapidly descended upon them. On September 16, the *Veslekari* docked at Alesund, Norway. The expedition was officially terminated—eighty days in voyage, with sixty days spent on East Greenland.

Louise was pleased by the trip. She had obtained a large botanical collection. Her training from Alice Eastwood had helped her to determine what specimens to bring home. She was also proud of her photogrammetrical surveys, and her success at using new methods in the field. The photogrammetry included three large-scale detailed maps of glaciers and a map of the hitherto unexplored Gregory Valley at the head of Franz Josef Fiord.

But it was her pictures of beautiful East Greenland, so isolated and difficult to travel to, that pleased Louise the most.

Chapter Six

Accolades and Adventure

Home. What a welcome sight after her many months away. Louise settled in at Maple Lawn, but not to rest. "The real work of an expedition begins when you return," she told friends. "I'm going to spend this winter and next summer studying our findings. You're an explorer even when you're home."

Her photographs needed to be developed and labeled. Botanical specimens had to be mounted, and then she needed to consult with Alice Eastwood. Louise also wanted to organize her notes and consult with the other expedition scientists. She organized a publication about the 1931 and 1933 expeditions to East Greenland for her sponsor, the American Geographical Society.

Reporters were fascinated by this woman who had traveled to places rarely visited by men. Usually, Louise graciously received their requests for interviews. Reporters always enjoyed talking to Louise because she was modest. They also loved her honesty, especially her ideas about femininity:

> As being the only woman in a corner of the world man still considers sacred, I may have worn breeches and boots and even slept in them at times, but I have no use for masculine women. At sea, I didn't bother with my hands, except to keep them from being frozen. But I powdered my nose before going on deck no matter how rough the sea was. There is no reason why a woman can't rough it and still remain feminine.

Constant invitations to speak about her adventures arrived at Maple Lawn. But Louise did not believe her accomplishments should be simply entertaining. She did, however, display her photographs and films at Maple Lawn for friends. As she readied the display, she felt it was "an excellent pictorial display of places that have probably never been visited."

The Fiord Region of East Greenland, Publication Number 18 was published by the American Geographical Society in 1935. Louise dedicated the book to her mother and father. J. Harlen Bretz, O. M. Miller, Walter A. Wood, and William B. Drew also contributed to the book. Louise selected 350 photographs from the thousands she took. She wrote the introductory narrative as well as explaining the details of the vessel and equipment.

Her work in East Greenland helped to develop several maps of the region. Three large-scale maps of the photogrammetrical surveys of Louise Glacier in Miss Boyd Land, Arch Glacier, and Moraineless Glacier in Gregory Valley were produced. Echo sounding maps and a bathymetric map of the floor of the Greenland Sea completed these works.

Louise had taken in stride her honor of having Miss Boyd Land and Louise Glacier named for her. Yet, to see her name on these important Arctic features gave her a sense of accomplishment. In 1943, the United States Board of Geographic Names decided to eliminate some of the marginal names on geographic features. The area charted by Louise's photographs continues to be officially recognized as "Miss Boyd Land."

Louise was honored when Dr. Isaiah Bowman encouraged her appointment as a delegate to the International Geographical Congress in Warsaw, Poland, in August 1934. She represented the United States government and the American Geographical Society.

Louise organized several small tours of the Polish countryside before the congress began. Always accustomed to luxury, she shipped her automobile and chauffeur to Poland for the tours. Then she invited Dr. Bowman and various Polish geographers to accompany her.

Dr. Bowman served as her photographic mentor on all the small excursions, helping her with any questions she had. Different geographers accompanied her as they drove through the Polish corridor, the Danzig Free State, and East Prussia. Louise chose each geographer for his regional expertise.

These excursions provided Louise with time for extensive photography. The old towns and ancient farms fascinated her. On one deeply rutted highway, she counted five hundred horse-drawn wagons, twenty-five pedestrians, and one bicycle in less than an hour. Louise respected the more primitive lifestyle, and was chagrined when her car frightened the horses.

Polish Countrysides was published in 1937 by the American Geographical Society. Louise illustrated it with almost 500 black and white photographs she took during her tour. The book is one of the best examples of rural Poland of the 1930s.

After spending time away from Arctic exploration, Louise wanted to continue what she most enjoyed. She planned her 1937 and 1938 expeditions together. Having laid the groundwork through previous voyages, she now knew the eastern coast of Greenland as well as any Arctic explorer alive. She had met danger and defied it, going further than any woman and few men. She was ready to continue the work of 1933.

Louise would travel farther north from the King Oscar and Franz Josef Fiord area than before. Her success depended on weather and ice conditions, so she allowed for flexibility. Louise knew that if adverse weather occurred, the expedition could always return to the King Oscar and Franz Josef Fiord region and continue projects there. The 1937 expedition would prepare Louise for the challenge of 1938—the northernmost expedition to date.

The American Geographical Society agreed to sponsor both projects, and Louise continued to finance them. She felt it was an excellent way to spend her money and contribute to the world's knowledge.

Louise again chose the *Veslekari* under the command of her good friend Captain Johan Olsen. After their previous trip she had great confidence in him, and the feeling was mutual. Although she was in charge, he knew she would defer many important decisions to him. She also was happy to have the same chief engineer aboard along with several of the 1933 crew. This crew understood the needs of the scientific staff, and good relationships continued.

Louise added a botanist with special interest in glacial plants to her scientific group. She knew plant life might tell a great deal about the effects of glacial recession. She also brought a hydrographer in charge of the sounding program and tide-gauge recording. Louise planned to

Women Here Are Preparing
For Voyages of Exploration

The *New York Times* celebrated Louise's successful Arctic expeditions in 1937.

make magnetic observations with equipment loaned by the U.S. Coast and Geodetic Survey Department. Louise would continue as the official photographer.

While the 1937 voyage went further north than previous ones and obtained new scientific data, it encountered delays and trouble from the beginning. Louise had hoped to start from Alesund, Norway, on June 1. But the sonic depth finder failed and she had to buy a new one. She sailed north along the Norwegian coast at a leisurely pace, planning to pick up the new depth finder in Narvik. Two weeks later, the depth finder was installed and they were ready to continue north to Tromsoe, Norway, to pick up the remaining expedition staff.

These delays meant they did not start across to Greenland until June 30, which distressed Louise. Not only did her plans for an early start fail, but heavy seas swept over the decks. The iron door of the galley had to remain closed to keep water from splashing on to the stove. Hip-length rubber boots were a necessity.

Their journey was so slow that although they had spotted the Greenland coast three days after starting through the ice, it took ten days to reach it. Although it was a long struggle, Louise still found the ice "fascinating and often beautiful. It gave one a good impression of what the true Far North is like and dispelled any idea that northeast Greenland is in all years easy of access."

In late July, they finally arrived at Young Sound, where land exploration was possible. Although it was 8:30 p.m., some expedition members went ashore as soon as the ship anchored. The late northern light allowed the scientists to take advantage of each hour. In the summer, the sun does not set until almost 11 p.m., and rises again around 2 a.m. Often the scientists worked fourteen hour days.

The next day, Louise and the hydrographer went by ship to the head of Tyroler Fiord. They hiked along the glaciers and valleys. Louise found an animal skin-covered hut, the first she had seen in Greenland. Eskimo hunters used the hut during the winter fox hunt. Along the way, they also saw many flowers in bloom. The musk oxen in the valley did not run at the sight of human beings. Instead, their menacing looks let Louise know this was their territory and they did not welcome intrusion.

Each morning the scientists waded ashore from rowboats. Then they tramped across the gravel delta, forded streams, and climbed into the high terminal moraines over loose rocks and stones. The hike became even more difficult in many places because of slippery ice.

After working hard each day, the return hike was along the same rough terrain. They had to cross Copeland Glacier that took from an hour-and-a-half to two hours. For future land explorations, Louise decided it was more logical to set up camp near the work.

The men were impressed by her hardiness. Later, one of the scientists commented that "you would hike miles each day for eight to twelve days....She could keep up with any man on those cross-country hikes."

Each evening when the scientists returned to the ship, they would go over the data they had collected, using an oil lamp for light. Louise set the pace for the men, saying later, "I'm reproached sometimes for wearing out the crew but they haven't suffered yet. There is never any hardship in doing what you are interested in."

By mid-August, ice conditions prevented them from continuing farther north. Louise was disappointed, yet happy their exploration yielded so much information. They turned south to once again explore Franz Josef Fiord and its adjacent areas. Ice became an extreme problem, keeping them three miles offshore from where they had landed without difficulty in 1933.

Louise was happy to return for the third time to familiar country. She looked forward to again seeing the 120 miles of the fiord's winding waterways. She noted fewer icebergs in Kjerulf Fiord than in 1931 and 1933— they were smaller and more broken up. They went ashore at the head of this fiord and set up camp for four days. Next, they visited the King Oscar Fiord region. Along the way they studied glaciers, and Louise continued to map the area with her photography.

Louise discovered a hut like this one on her 1937 expedition. The animal skin-covered shelter served to house Eskimo hunters.

Soon, ice and bad weather threatened the expedition. Captain Olsen was apprehensive. The drifting pack ice in the fiord indicated winter would set in earlier than usual. Later, Louise realized that the captain had no idea the season was going to close in so quickly.

On August 23, Captain Olsen ordered Louise and the expedition crew to finish their work that day. The weather was beautiful, and the staff wondered at the haste. They were all aboard, however, by half past six that evening and ready to sail.

Two days out they encountered drifting ice. Captain Olsen told Louise the size of the floes suggested difficulties ahead. Soon, they encountered thick, tight ice. Ten hours later, they had only gone three miles. As far as Captain Olsen could see from the crow's nest, heavy polar ice fields and floes blocked the coast. He told Louise heavy polar ice had come south and its movement had closed the coast for miles. He moved the ship whenever he found the slightest opening, but it was in vain.

On August 25, their worst fears were realized. The ship was pinched by the ice and tipped several degrees on her side. Captain Olsen ordered the crew to use dynamite, which broke the ice and righted the ship undamaged. By morning, the ice had slackened a little and they were able to make some progress. But at the end of two hours, they again were blocked by large ice floes that reached to the coast. Captain Olsen told Louise that sailing onward seemed impossible.

"Would the ice change?" Louise asked, "And can we afford to wait on the chance it might do so?"

"There is no possibility of getting back into Franz Josef Fiord," the captain said. "The passage we came through just a few hours previously is now completely closed."

Louise and Captain Olsen discussed the situation with the staff and crew. They decided the only alternative was to go one hundred miles out of the way to King Oscar Fiord and then south to the sea. They had enough coal, so they moved forward. When they arrived at King Oscar Fiord, however, they found heavy ice. There were no open leads through which they could move. "But," said Captain Olsen, "we have to keep moving."

It was a struggle against time. Two dangers loomed before them: The ice might close in so tightly they would be unable to get out that season, or worse, the ship might be beset in the heavy ice and crushed.

All hands were pressed into service—scientific staff included. They manned the ice anchors, leaping from floe to floe with the heavy equipment and hammering the anchors into the ice, which gave the ship leverage. Many of the floes were fifteen feet above the sea, as high as the *Veslekari*'s bow.

Captain Olsen commanded operations from the crow's

nest. Hot coffee and food were on hand at all times in the crew's galley. There were no regular meals. Louise and the men snatched food when they could.

No one slept, and Louise was on deck all night. There was one brief respite when they found a small lead between the ice and the shore at Antarctic Harbor. But soon they were in heavy ice again. The progress the next day was no less difficult.

Late that afternoon, some light snow fell and fog developed. The floes began to diminish in size. By midnight they were through them to the open coast. The point where they started their detour was only 120 miles away. It had been a long and desperate journey.

As they left King Oscar Fiord, more heavy pack ice blocked the shore, extending out to sea for thirty-five miles. There was open water between the floes. They were able to get out of the ice and sail for Norway on August 29. A shout went up in relief.

Chapter Seven

Northernmost Landing

After the 1937 voyage, Louise's reputation for hard work grew. Her devotion to detail had impressed both the scientists and the ship's crew, who saw not a wealthy woman indulging herself, but a sincere explorer. More than anything, they appreciated her willingness to do the same jobs any other crewmember had to do.

Louise intended to go as far north through the ice as possible in 1938. She asked some staff members to return and hired new ones. The hydrographer and surveyor returned. She asked F. Eyolf Bronner, a geologist, and radio expert A. F. Hilferty to accompany her. The radio equipment had been designed specifically for Louise to be used for experiments as well as communication. Louise decided to do the botanical collecting herself and would later confirm the species with Alice Eastwood.

All members of the expedition were at port and the ship was ready to sail on June 1, earlier than on any previous trips. Louise was excited, hardly able to wait. But the echo sounding equipment failed on the trial run. Once again, they had to postpone until it was in working condition. On June 8, they sailed from Alesund, Norway, to test the echo sounder. After it was fixed, they began the expedition on June 13, 1938.

They arrived at Jan Mayen Island ahead of schedule, twenty days earlier than in 1937 and twenty-two days earlier than in 1933. Louise was satisfied. It looked like the expedition would be more successful than any previous one.

Louise and the crew again delivered mail and newspapers to the men stationed on the island. Captain Olsen and the hydrographer wanted to observe tides and currents and take soundings, so Louise allowed them a few extra days. Going ashore with two assistants, Louise walked for hours high above the bay. She loved the wild appearance of the country as they crossed water-soaked ground and tramped over thick moss. The day was raw and bitterly cold. When the fog became thick, moisture froze on the twill of Louise's hiking pants.

On July 14, the *Veslekari* started north. No large fields of ice appeared until July 16. At this point, the ship already had reached 81 degrees 30 minutes. They went northeast to Spitsbergen and planned to cross from there to Greenland, sailing as far north as possible. Once they reached the island, they journeyed west in thick fog. The Greenland coast was sighted on July 25, exactly a year since their first landing in 1937. This time, ice had not impeded them. They traveled further north than before.

In Copeland Fiord, Louise explored in the motor dory for two days. She was fascinated with the almost vertical walls and their striking, colorful formations. A large valley to the south was filled with exceptionally rich vegetation.

On July 31, Louise and Captain Olsen decided to move to the coast and sail north. They did not stop as they made their way out of the fiord. The sounder worked continuously, gathering detailed information.

Just when Captain Olsen thought all was well, tight ice engulfed them. Olsen managed to work the ship through. By the time they reached the east coast of Shannon Island, they saw only small ice floes. Plenty of open water spread before them.

As they continued northward, they traveled waters rarely open for ships. Only a narrow strip of pack ice lined the shore, and some small, drifting ice floes littered the sea around the ship. They approached a strip of polar ice that rimmed the shore. It was much wider than what they had seen before, and there was no possibility of getting through it to land. Icebergs rose out of the ice and the land was covered with more snow. The 120 mile wide entrance to Skaer Fiord was completely blocked when they passed. The *Veslekari* had entered the outer reaches of the navigable Arctic.

As they continued, they passed heavy polar ice packed solid as far as they could see. They sailed between Cape Amelie and the west side of Ile de France, where ships had never traveled. They kept drifting in the ice through the night and early morning of August 3, hoping it would change. Louise wanted to continue northward. By the next morning, it was obvious they had gone as far north as they could go. They were at 77 degrees 48 minutes north latitude. The North Pole was only 800 miles away.

Captain Olsen anchored to a field of polar ice that was grounded and frozen to the shore. The ice was as high as the bow of the ship, fifteen feet above the water. Many hummocks were even higher.

Anxious to explore, Louise and the others climbed a ladder from the ship to the ice, then inched their way over the ice's rough surface to land. They crossed heaps of rock debris that had been pushed up where the ice field butted against the shore and formed strange patterns above their heads.

Streams of melt water flowed from the icecap. They had to flounder knee-deep through a wide strip of mud to get from the ice to dry land. The higher slopes of the island below the icecap were fairly hard-surfaced and

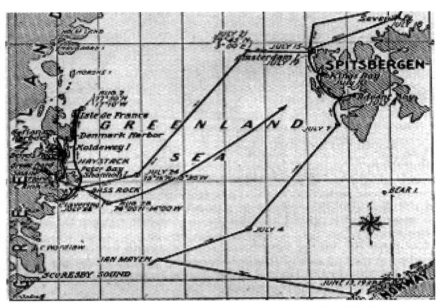

Louise's 1938 expedition followed this route, bringing the explorer within 800 miles of the North Pole.

vegetation grew sparsely in small clumps.

To the best of Louise's knowledge, theirs was the farthest north landing ever made on the east coast of Greenland. If they had only arrived one or two days earlier, she thought, they might have been able to go further north. Not only did the ice fields block their way, but the fields were already drifting south.

Captain Olsen did not want to risk getting caught in the southbound ice fields. He asked Louise and the scientists to make their trip ashore a quick one. He wanted to leave in open water. They granted his wish and were ready to sail by four o'clock in the afternoon.

The ship went southeast through the ice for a short time, then southwest. Louise was ecstatic. All she had wished to do on this journey had been accomplished. While ashore, she had spent profitable hours with her cameras. She continued shooting pictures from the deck of the ship. She wanted to record as much as possible of this seldom-visited coast.

The mountains and high cliffs she so loved in East Greenland had been replaced by a rather flat and regular shoreline. She was photographing views no other photographer had ever shot, and she was thrilled to be contributing to the world's knowledge of the Arctic.

As they returned south, they met no resistance from ice. Louise and her staff spent the remainder of the time surveying, photographing, and collecting. She was especially excited about the plants she found.

Louise also noted that one year from the day when they began their battle through the ice in King Oscar Fiord, they had no difficulties as they left the coast.

On September 7, Louise sent a wireless dispatch to the *New York Times.* An article appeared on September 9 along with a map of the expedition's route and a photograph of Louise in her fur-lined parka. The dateline read: "Louise A. Boyd Arctic Expedition on the Steamship *Veslekari.*" The article was accompanied by a story by Dr.

John K. Wright of the American Geographical Society, who said,

> Miss Boyd may claim the credit of having gone farther north in a ship along the East Greenland shore than any other American and of having attained what is probably the second highest latitude ever reached by a vessel in these waters.

Chapter Eight

A Dash in Time

When Louise returned home, she was fifty-one years old and had no idea what her next adventure would be. "I don't know that I'll ever go into the Arctic again," she said, "but if anyone told me I never could go, I think I'd start North again right now."

As she settled into life at Maple Lawn and her San Francisco home in Pacific Heights, Louise returned to her old routine. Once again she became a committee member of the San Francisco Symphony Orchestra. She organized the American Woman's Volunteer Association in San Rafael. And, she got her finances in order.

Maple Lawn required her attention. Her magnolia trees needed pruning and her azaleas and camellias tending. Her camellias were the finest privately-owned collection in the United States. With her gardening expertise, she always was in demand to speak to garden groups.

Mills College in Oakland asked her to become a trustee

in 1941. *Who's Who in America* listed her in the 1940-1941 edition.

As in the 1920s, Louise became the hostess of fabulous Christmas parties. Maple Lawn was brightly lit with a huge Christmas tree, and the aroma of hot pecan punch filled the hall.

After the guests had arrived, Louise would walk slowly down the huge staircase. "Merry Christmas," she called out in her raspy voice. The men received a present, usually a necktie. Sometimes the more important officials received a check.

Although her social life took up time now, Louise made her Arctic research a priority. Her goal was simply to compile her research. She continued to work with Alice Eastwood, who was impressed with Louise's newest specimens. Louise separated and labeled her photographs and decided what to publish.

She received recognition for her expeditions. The American Geographical Society honored her with its highest award—the Cullum Geographical Medal. She was the second woman the society had so honored in its eighty-six year history. Inscribed on the medal was the praise: "The dauntless leader of scientific expeditions into the Arctic, she has captured the spirit of the polar world in photographs of rare beauty."

Her fame also was proclaimed in headlines. One article

said she was "the only woman to achieve an outstanding position in Arctic exploration." But, as she entered the American spotlight, always wearing a camellia on her shoulder, problems loomed ahead.

When Louise started her 1938 expedition, she knew Europe was changing, and not for the good. Already, Hitler had annexed Austria, and in 1939, he attacked Poland. By 1940, Denmark, Norway, The Netherlands, and Belgium were also under siege.

These invasions posed a direct threat to the Danish territory of Greenland and to the Norwegian territories of Jan Mayen Island and Spitsbergen. Events looked grim. The arrival of American troops in Iceland in 1941 proved the strategic importance of the Arctic to the United States government.

With World War II in focus, the American Geographical Society asked Louise to postpone publication of her 1937 and 1938 findings. They feared her work could provide the enemy with critical knowledge that would help them mount attacks. She agreed.

Then Louise was faced with infuriating news. After her 1938 journey, Louise had left most of her equipment in Alesund, Norway, because she had anticipated another journey. She learned that all of her cameras, radios, sounding equipment, scientific equipment, canoes, and Arctic clothing had been impounded by German soldiers after their invasion of Oslo. Furious, she arranged a trip from New York to the Norwegian capital.

Louise would be safe from capture because the United States was not at war with Germany. Still, she was concerned about the condition of her equipment and cameras—or if she would even find them.

When she arrived in Alesund, Louise found her possessions intact. She had them loaded on the ship, and sailed home on a luxury liner. Aboard, she met Dr. J. H. Dellinger, who was head of the radio section of the National Bureau of Standards. As they talked, he recognized a true Arctic expert.

She had been lucky in her timing. Soon after returning home, the United States entered the war with Germany. Had Louise waited, her hopes to regain her equipment would have been shattered, and she would probably not have been allowed to return home. She was simply too valuable: the Germans would have had a great interest in capturing one of the foremost experts on the Arctic.

When she returned to San Rafael, the city gave a huge party for her. City officials recognized the distinction she brought to San Rafael through her work. They acknowledged their pride in her accomplishments by making her an honorary citizen of the city. Tribute after tribute followed. A friend said, "Her friends hold her not as a famous person but as a woman great in spirit." Another friend put it more simply: "She's a darn swell person."

Louise was overwhelmed by the comments. Later she said, "No recognition from any foreign country brought me the happiness my friends and neighbors provided by giving a reception and dinner for me." Louise anticipated settling down until World War II ended. She had no idea of the next adventure coming her way.

Chapter Nine

Serving Her Country

The United States government desperately needed Louise's expertise in its war with Germany. For years the Danes and Norwegians had been the only explorers in the Arctic. They had set up wireless stations and weather stations. But the U.S. did not even have a consul in Greenland until 1941. "Information regarding Northeast Greenland prior to our entering the war was extremely scanty," wrote Rear Admiral Edward H. Smith, U.S. Coast Guard. The U.S. had no explorers or scientists on equal scale with their Northern European counterparts—except for Louise.

Rear Admiral Edward H. Smith, nicknamed "Iceberg" because of his expertise in ice navigation, was preparing a mission to Northeast Greenland in the summer of 1940. When Dr. J. H. Dellinger returned to Washington, D. C., he told Smith about Louise's Arctic expertise. Smith decided to consult her.

Louise met Rear Admiral Smith in Washington, D. C.,

to answer questions about Greenland and the Arctic. Smith was overwhelmed by the abundant, helpful data she provided. "Voluminous photographs, including splendid panoramic views of important headlands and assistance in identifying topographic features," he wrote. Her information was of "great assistance in the navigation of these little known ice-infested waters."

Louise stayed in Washington, D. C., through the fall at the official request of the Bureau of Standards. Proud that her knowledge was so important to her government, she spent hours discussing the Arctic with bureau administrators. Soon the bureau realized it needed more information.

"Why not an expedition north?" Louise suggested. She was eager to return. Louise was granted authorization for the journey from the Carnegie Institute and the radio section of the Bureau of Standards. This time she would go to the Arctic of Eastern Canada and West Greenland. She agreed to charter a boat and finance the official expedition in the summer of 1941.

The "official" purpose of the expedition was to obtain data about long-distance radio transmission in the Arctic, particularly of ionospheric conditions. The bureau had developed portable ionosphere equipment that they used in Texas and Brazil during solar eclipses. They had no data, however, from points in the Arctic region.

But this was only a front: Louise was actually part of a secret mission. At a monthly meeting of the Society of Woman Geographers in Washington, D. C., Louise confided that "the route of the expedition and other details will not be made public."

As with previous expeditions, chartering a ship, hiring a crew, and buying food and supplies were Louise's responsibility. The Bureau of Standards arranged for the scientists and their equipment.

Louise chartered the schooner *Effie M. Morrissey.* She knew the ship's captain, the legendary Robert Abram Bartlett. Captain "Bob" Bartlett, was "a real salt." At sixty-six years old, he had been in the expedition business for years. Born in Newfoundland, Bob spoke with a crisp Irish brogue, had traveled everywhere, and was well-versed in history.

In 1897, he started accompanying Robert E. Peary on various expeditions. On the final Peary trip, Bartlett led the last support party that Peary sent back before he made his final dash for the North Pole. Bartlett had commanded expeditions to North Greenland, northwest Alaska, Ellesmere Island, the west shore of Baffin Island, Siberia, and Labrador. He was regarded as one of the great ice navigators of all time, and he had a strong personality to go with it.

Bartlett was not impressed with Louise "being a

woman." He gave Louise the same cabin he had fixed for Marie Peary Stafford when she sailed with him to Greenland to dedicate a monument to her father.

Bartlett's ship had a personality, too. The *Effie M. Morrissey* was a small, coal-black, two-masted schooner. Bartlett had commanded her on fifteen previous expeditions. The schooner was built of oak planking and green sheathing. Launched in 1894, her length was one hundred four feet, and she was twenty-three feet wide. She had been used before for scientific exploration.

Louise was now fifty-five years old and accustomed to running her own expedition. This would be her ninth journey into the Arctic. Furthermore, she was financing the expedition and would not be taken for granted. Louise would not have her authority questioned. She realized Barlett's strong personality might clash with her determination, but she saw no other way to make this journey. He was an expert seaman. She would make the best of it.

Before leaving, Louise attended a luncheon in her honor. Instead of her knowledge of the Arctic, one reporter was impressed with the explorer's attire:

> She's tall and slender and looks a little bit as I have always imagined the young Queen of Alexandria of England must have looked. But

despite the fact that Miss Louise Boyd looks like the woman who set the fashions of an era...and has a transparent, lovely complexion...she's far from the fragile flowers of that period.

Louise had worn a tall hat with white taffeta bows, a navy and white printed frock, a diamond and pearl dog-collar, and a number of very handsome rings on her slender fingers. She also wore deep red polish on per-fectly manicured nails.

She was quick to explain that she did not use nail polish while aboard ship. "But I always use lipstick no matter where I am. And I take very good care of my skin. Those northern glares of sun on ice can play havoc with it if you don't keep it properly creamed and softened."

At 5:40 p.m. on June 1, 1941, the *Morrissey* started its journey from a pier near the War Department in Wash-ington, D. C. Louise waved to friends on the pier. The four scientists aboard chatted among themselves. Bartlett and his crew of eleven busily attended their duties.

The schooner sailed up the west coast of Greenland, then returned by the coast of Baffin Island and Labrador. As usually occurred on these far north journeys, weather became a major factor.

They were battered by a one hundred-mile-per-hour gale and sixty-foot waves. Anything not battened down was thrown in the storm, including members of the party. No one knew if the ship would survive in the violent wind. But no one panicked, least of all Louise.

Her strong attitude surprised Captain Bartlett, even though he resented their equal status on the expedition. He felt she was an upstart in the polar explorer club. Whenever possible, he would try to ignore her. When he could not, he would only listen halfheartedly.

Although Louise sensed his coolness, she did not allow it to bother her and showed him no emotion. Afterward, she never mentioned their relationship to any of her friends. Some mused that with their strong personalities, Bartlett and Louise might have been attracted to one another. Louise, however, never acknowledged these rumors.

The expedition had been a total success. As reported in the *Technical News Bulletin* of the Bureau of Standards, "The Government is indebted to Miss Boyd for her effective leadership of the expedition and is gratified with the results achieved." Louise had gathered geographical information to aid the government in the war effort.

One military officer wrote to Louise, "Your work with us has been invaluable. You have given the War Department a trunk-full of original maps, charts and pictures which provide very essential data. Your industry, accuracy and long background of scientific exploration enable you to make a major contribution."

Louise was proud of her knowledge and the success of the trip: "I knew every inch and since the maps and photographs belonging to Denmark were in German hands, my memory and my own surveys were the only guides the Allies had."

In interviews, however, she continued to dismiss her adventure as she had in previous years. She acted like someone who merely had been traveling—not making a historic journey. After her return, she continued to serve the U.S. government—for the fee of one dollar a year. Many experts volunteered their services during World War II for this amount. Louise was the first woman to join the government staff in this capacity.

Louise served as special consultant to the Military Intelligence Division from March 1942 to July 1943. She took her consulting position very seriously, and was careful to maintain confidentiality. She even bought stationery printed with her title: "Expert Consultant for the U.S. Government."

In late summer, Louise returned to Maple Lawn. She was relieved to be home. After World War II ended, she was presented with a Certificate of Appreciation from the Army, "For outstanding patriotic service to the Army as a contributor of geographic knowledge and consultant."

Chapter Ten

Living Life to the Fullest

Louise believed that money was meant to be spent, and she did it lavishly, whether entertaining at home or traveling with friends. After World War II, Louise redecorated Maple Lawn and resumed her old social life. She attended social events in San Francisco and Pacific Heights and served on the Board of Directors of charitable organizations.

On the east side of the house she built a banquet-size dining room that would seat forty guests. On the west side, she added a huge living room and library to display the mementos and maps of her expeditions. She adorned the walls with photographs of royalty as well as heads of state who had sent their personal greetings. She loved nothing more than to show her guests her memorabilia, especially from her journeys in the 1930s. In addition, Louise had all the rugs and draperies removed and the walls and ceilings cleaned and repainted. One look at her kitchen convinced her to modernize it.

Her cook decided to return to China to live out the rest of his life. He had worked for Louise and her family for fifty years. While she hated to see him go, she understood his desire to return to his homeland, and she supported him for the rest of his life. New cooks took his place, but never quite satisfied her as he had done.

She began another major renovation outdoors. A porte-cochere was built over the front steps that extended from the front door of the house over the adjacent driveway. Visitors could walk from their cars to the house in all weather. She moved a forty-five-foot fir tree from the San Rafael firehouse at a cost of two thousand dollars.

Louise built a two-level structure that housed a swimming pool and terrace garden. The lower level contained a glass-enclosed card room and a stone marquee for serving buffets. The upper level contained the swimming pool. She also designed a glass-enclosed living room and fully equipped kitchen. She also built a sauna—a treat she encountered in Scandinavia.

Her gardens had a reputation for beauty throughout the San Francisco Bay Area. People often visited Maple Lawn to view her colorful display. Louise gave much of the credit to her gardener, Ah Sing, who had cared for the Boyd gardens for over fifty years. Ah Sing also returned to China when he retired. As with her cook, Louise would support him for the rest of his life.

Louise now had more time for her pet project, camellias, which she grew in wood lath houses at the rear of the property. She also grew a cutting garden for fresh flowers. Louise insisted upon having fresh flowers available at all times. Tending her camellias and azaleas gave her contentment only matched by her Arctic journeys. Many times, strangers approached her at public events to say hello, recognizing her by the huge camellia she always wore on her shoulder.

Constant visitors came to Maple Lawn—enjoying the pool, the gardens, and Louise's company. Her warmth and caring, more than her money, drew people to her. Reporters always commented on her charm, "which attracts everyone who meets her." Marjorie Fountain, whose husband, Gordan Fountain, accompanied Admiral Richard Byrd on his 1933-1935 expedition, said, "We used to have the most marvelous parties at Maple Lawn."

As her hair turned silver, Louise became even lovelier. She retained her regal stance and trim figure. Everyone still noticed when she entered a room.

Louise believed her wealth gave her additional responsibilities to her community. Among her many civic activities, she served as president of the Marin Music Chest. This group raised money for scholarships for young musicians. She donated $19,000 to an art group called the San Francisco Foundation. Cultural and civic groups in

Marin County and San Francisco knew they always could count on Louise Arner Boyd.

San Francisco Magazine named Louise one of the Grande Dames of the city. She usually bought three Grand Tier seats for the Opera or Symphony and attended with a married couple. The San Francisco Ballet had her continued support.

Louise loved automobiles. Never having learned to drive herself, she depended on her chauffeurs. One of her unusual cars was a Locomobile, even more expensive and prestigious than a Cadillac at that time. Nothing was more pleasurable for her than to telephone her Marin County friends and say, "L.A.B. [Louise Arner Boyd] will be over to pick you up in the Loco."

One evening, after a party in Pacific Heights, her chauffeur held open the door of her 1957 Packard formal sedan. Elegantly, she entered the back seat and settled herself—dress carefully placed, hat removed. Happily, she looked out the window and waved. Her chauffeur started the car. With a roar he accelerated down the street and up a hill. Louise's hair and scarf blew out the open window. Her friends stared in amazement until one said, "That's Louise. She has an exit as dramatic as her entrances!" Louise encouraged her chauffeurs to drive fast all the time.

Both Mills College and the University of California

at Berkeley presented Louise with honorary degrees, but she always laughed when someone referred to her as "doctor." "I'm just me," she would say.

Yet, she did greet visitors wearing two ribbons. One held the colors of the French Legion of Honor; the other the blue and white of the Order of St. Olaf of Norway. She was proud to display these honors, reminiscent of her aid during the search for Amundsen.

She also was a Fellow of the Royal Geographical Society of London, of the American Society of Photogrammetry, and of the American Geophysical Society.

In 1948, the American Geographical Society published Louise's book, *The Coast of Northeast Greenland, Publication Number 30*, that had been on hold until after the war.

As a reporter watched this tall, slim, modish woman move among guests at a fashionable Georgetown residence in Washington, D.C., she realized Louise "was doing what she wanted to do with her life and enjoying it." Before she retired, however, Louise had one more challenge to fulfill—to reach the North Pole.

Although she had approached within 800 miles of the North Pole, she wanted to actually go "over the top." She also believed her previous scientific work would not be complete without photographs of this spot.

In June 1955, she hired a plane to become the first

woman to fly over the North Pole. She would carry the flag of the Society of Woman Geographers—and the best wishes of all her friends. Hers was the first privately financed flight over the Pole.

Louise never liked airplane flight, but at sixty-eight years old, it was the only way she could reach her dream. She chartered a DC-4 and crew: captain, copilot, two navigators, and one engineer. At the beginning of the trip, Louise kept a detailed diary.

Leaving June 12, she wrote: "The captain told us we flew over Nantucket which we could not see because of clouds. Flew at 7,000 feet." At 10:20 p.m., she wrote, "woke up at Goose Bay, Labrador. Brilliant stars out. Smooth landing." Louise and the crew slept at Goose Bay and then were off again.

As they readied the plane for the North Pole flight, Louise thought about when she was a little girl. She had dreamed of going to the North Pole. Now the time had come. On June 16, 1955, they took off from Bodo, Norway. She wrote:

> North, north, north we flew. Soon we left all land behind us. From the cabin window I saw great stretches of ocean flecked with patches of white floating ice. Now the ice became denser, its jagged edges surrounding open pools of sea. And as I saw the ocean change to massive fields of

solid white, my heart leaped up. I knew we were approaching my goal. Then—in a moment of happiness which I shall never forget—our instruments told me we were there. For directly below us, 9,000 feet down, lay the North Pole! No cloud in the brilliant blue sky hid our view of this glorious field of shining ice. Suddenly I felt we had an invisible passenger—the Almighty. In a moment of silence and reverent awe the crew and I gave thanks for this priceless sight. We crossed the Pole, then circled it, flying "around the world" in a matter of minutes. Then we departed. My Arctic dream had come true.

Chapter Eleven

Final Years

Although her Arctic adventures had ceased, Louise remained active. She continued to travel in California and throughout the world, spending four to five months each year abroad. In the spring of 1958, she embarked on a tour through Japan, Hong Kong, Macao, Saigon, Bangkok, Cambodia, Kashmir, Pakistan, through the Khyber Pass into Afghanistan, and Turkey.

The mysteries of other countries and especially their people appealed to her—and she always wanted to know more. She kept diaries of several trips—from Portugal in 1926 to The Netherlands in 1955.

Louise became an honorary member of the American Polar Society. She was the first woman to become a member and only one of seven others to gain this recognition. Her award read "for conspicuous achievement in the rugged realm of Arctic endeavor."

When presenting the award, the speaker commented

that Miss Boyd "contributed more to our knowledge of Greenland, Spitsbergen, Franz Josef Land and the Greenland Sea than has the work of any other explorer."

Louise attended Polar Society meetings. Some of her closest friends were members of the society, and she served as a director for twelve years. Members loved Louise, whom they considered gentle and bright-eyed.

Marjorie Fountain remembered Louise "enjoyed life and was always willing to go on an expedition or attend a party. She never allowed anything to stand in her way."

Louise learned the *Veslekari* had gone down in ice in Newfoundland. She wrote to a friend, "I am going out to dinner tonight, with an awful feeling of sadness for I feel as if I have lost one of my best friends when I think that the *Veslekari* has gone down in the Atlantic. I love that ship and all she meant to me and enabled me to do."

She wrote to the company where she chartered the vessel. A company spokesperson wrote back, referring to the two books Louise had compiled from research done on the ship: "I understand well that you were sorry when you saw *Veslekari*'s breakdown. She went down with the flag at the top. It was a good vessel and it is the only vessel that has got a whole book of 270 pages and 68 fotos."

In 1960, Louise became the first woman in the 108 year history of the American Geographical Society to be elected to the chief policy-making body of the society.

Louise Arner Boyd received awards and honors for arctic exploration throughout her life.

When notified at Maple Lawn, she said "I am kind of flabbergasted. I consider it a signal honor to be named to such a post." At that time, the society had over 4000 members consisting of professional geographers, explorers, and educators. "I am especially honored to become the first woman to receive such recognition," she said. "I will be so happy to see another woman similarly honored in the future." Then she added, "I'm going to do my level best to make good on that job. I've kept up all my interests in geography and exploration, and I'm determined to make this position my principal work from now on."

At seventy-two years old, she speculated on her exploration career. She felt she was "lucky" to have entered the field when explorers worked without wireless apparatus, carried their equipment on their backs, and broke their own trails.

"It's a highly organized business now," she said. "They've got radio, submarines, airplanes and helicopters—and it's much too complicated and expensive for the small expeditions. I'm afraid I wouldn't be able to conduct explorations today as I and others did thirty years ago."

The Louise Boyd Junior Museum in San Rafael was named after her. The California Academy of Sciences made her an honorary member. In 1969, she flew to Fairbanks, Alaska, to receive an honorary degree in science from the University of Alaska. During this trip, she flew to Point Barrow to participate in a ceremony opening a Naval Arctic Research Laboratory.

But life had started to catch up with this vibrant woman in 1962. Whether she made mistakes in managing her fortune, or others took advantage of her, is only speculation. Perhaps she simply had spent too much money on her expeditions and trips. Whatever the reason, her huge fortune had dwindled.

She sold her house in Pacific Heights and moved to a small apartment on San Francisco's Nob Hill. Maple Lawn and its sprawling grounds had to go. The Elks Club of San Rafael bought the property in 1962 for $350,000. They gave her a lifetime membership—but her friends doubted she ever would want to return.

Her fine furniture, Danish china, and all her other possessions were auctioned off by Butterfield and Butterfield. Fortunately, photographs of the beautiful mansion remain thanks to the photographer Ansel Adams.

Ever efficient, Louise donated her library of Arctic and Scandinavian books to the Universities of Alaska and California. Her books on California wildflowers and natural science went to the Louise Boyd Natural Science Museum in San Rafael. All her work for the American Geographical Society is located in the Golda Meir Library, University of Wisconsin, Milwaukee.

She continued to visit with friends and work on civic

boards. In 1967, at age eighty, she attended the annual Explorer's Club dinner in New York City. The *New Yorker* reported she arrived "in a pink dress festooned with white orchids." At the dinner she was introduced as "one of the world's greatest woman explorers."

Louise's health, however, was rapidly deteriorating. She had a series of operations for intestinal cancer and was unable to continue her frantic pace. She first ignored her physician's warnings and continued to travel, but soon it became impossible.

When Louise moved to a nursing home in San Francisco, she was so financially strapped that friends helped support her. Each day at noon, Marjorie Fountain went from her job in the financial district to the nursing home to be sure Louise was eating.

Her friends did not allow Louise to be alone during her final days. They wanted to make her last days peaceful and happy, giving to her as she had given to them.

On September 14, 1972, just two days before she turned eighty-five years old, Louise died.

Friends mourned more than the passing of a great woman. They mourned the person who cared so much about them, who enjoyed a good time, who contributed personally and monetarily to the world's knowledge: "...you couldn't overlook her. She was a vivid personality and the life of the many parties she hosted."

Although her funeral was held at St. Paul's Episcopal Church in San Rafael, no burial took place. She wanted her ashes scattered over the Arctic regions, particularly Miss Boyd Land. Unfortunately, the cost prohibited this, so the ashes were scattered 100 miles north of Point Barrow, the last place she visited in the Arctic.

No grave or plaque exists in San Rafael to commemorate her life and contributions, but she will never be forgotten in that city. A special room in the Marin County Historical Society celebrates her life.

Louise Arner Boyd was a legendary figure. A news article commented, "Miss Boyd decided that being an heiress wasn't enough to fill one's life especially if one had the adventuresome blood of do-and-daring ancestors in one's makeup." The Reverend Hugh Hardin added in his eulogy: "She possessed a freedom that too many of us are afraid to exercise."

That is the beauty of Louise Arner Boyd's life. She was an explorer and a socialite—and she was truly the heroine of the Arctic.

Timeline

1887—Louise Arner Boyd born on September 16.

1901—Seth Boyd dies of rheumatic fever.

1902—John Boyd, Jr. dies of rheumatic fever.

1909—Becomes president and manager of the Boyd Investment Company.

1919—Louise's mother, Louise Arner Boyd, dies in a nursing home.

1920—Louise's father, John Franklin Boyd, dies. Louise inherits her parents' fortune.

1921—Travels to Europe.

1924—Travels to Spitsenberg, Norway, in the Arctic Sea.

1925—Presented to King George V and Queen Mary at the Court of St. James on June 29.

1926—Charters the *Hobby* to make first Arctic journey.

1928—Postpones scientific expedition in order to join the search for Roald Amundsen and his crew. Receives the Order of St. Olaf from the Norwegian government and the Chevalier of the Legion of Honor from France.

1931—Visits Franz Josef and King Oscar Fiords on the East Greenland coast aboard the *Veslekari*. Discovers De Geer Glacier. Miss Boyd Land is named for her.

1934—Travels to Warsaw, Poland, as a delegate to the International Geographical Congress in August.

1937—First attempt to travel north from Franz Josef and King Oscar Fiords aboard the *Veslekari*.

1938—Travels within 800 miles of the North Pole aboard the *Veslekari*.

1939—Hurries to Alesund, Norway, to retrieve equipment from German troops.

1941—Charters the *Effie M. Morrissey* to head a military intelligence secret mission in the Arctic Sea.

1942—Serves as Special Consultant to the Military Intelligence Division of the United States Government.

1955—Becomes the first woman to fly over the North Pole on June 16.

1958—Tours Asia.

1960—Becomes first woman elected to the chief policy-making body of the American Geographical Society.

1972—Dies in a nursing home in San Francisco, California. Louise Arner Boyd's ashes are spread 100 miles north of Point Barrow, Alaska, the last place she visited in the Arctic.

Bibliography

Books

Cain, Ella M. *The Story of Early Mono County.* San Francisco: Fearon Publishers, Inc., 1961.

Loose, Warren. *The Bodie Bonanza.* Jericho, New York: Exposition Press, Inc., 1971.

Moss, Jocelyn. "The Call of the Arctic: Travels of Louise Boyd." *Marin County Historical Society Magazine,* Vol. XIV, Number 2, 1987.

Olds, Elizabeth Fagg. *Women of the Four Winds: The Adventures of Four of America's First Women Explorers.* Boston: Houghton Mifflin Company, 1985.

Wedertz, Frank S. *Bodie 1859-1900.* Bishop, California: Chalfant Press, Inc., 1969.

Wick, Marilyn. "From Bodie to B Street: The Making of the Boyd Fortune" *Marin County Historical Society Magazine,* Vol. XIV, No. 2, 1987.

Scrapbooks and Diaries by Louise Arner Boyd (Provided by Marin County Historical Society.)

Portugal 1926
Finland 1930

Plants/Flowers Jan Mayen Island Greenland 1931
Amsterdam 1955
Holland 1955
Flight over the North Pole 1955
Sweden (date unknown)

Books and Articles by Louise Arner Boyd

The Fiord Region of East Greenland, Special *Publication, no.*
18, American Geographical Society, 1935.
Polish Countrysides, Special Publication, no. 20, American
Geographical Society, 1937.
The Coast of Northeast Greenland, Special Publication, no. 30,
American Geographical Society, 1948.
"A view from 9,000 feet," *Parade Magazine,* 1955.

Personal Interviews

Marjorie Fountain, Oakland, California: She and her husband
Gordan were close friends of Louise, having met in the Polar
Society. She provided the delightful details of Louise's strong
personality and generous nature.

Sources

CHAPTER ONE

p. 9, "I was a tomboy..." "Marin Woman Who 'tamed Arctic.' " *San Rafael Independent*. March 9, 1981.

p. 12, "born geographer..." ibid.

CHAPTER TWO

p. 20, "When I do anything..." *New York World Telegram*. May 12, 1924.

p. 22, "Someday I want..." *San Francisco Magazine*. December 1984, p. 41 ff.

p. 22, "best training," ibid.

p. 25, "...isolation combined with danger..." "San Rafael Woman Feted by Fellow Citizens for Outstanding Achievements." *San Rafael Independent*. January 6, 1939.

CHAPTER THREE

p. 28, "How could I go..." "American Woman Searching for Amundsen." *New York Herald*. August 9, 1928.

p. 30, "We returned here..." ibid.

p. 31, "Folks here think..." *San Rafael Independent*. November 21, 1928.

CHAPTER FOUR

p. 40, "were sad to see these...." Boyd, Louise Arner. *The Fiord Region of East Greenland, Special Publication, no. 18.* American Geographical Society, 1935.

CHAPTER FIVE

p. 43, "We shall do as much..." "Woman Leader of Explorers." *London Daily Mail.* June 9, 1933.

p. 44, "A slight error of judgement..." Boyd, Louise Arner. *The Fiord Region...* op. cit.

p. 46, "as if we were..." op. cit.

p. 48, "I've confined the fire..." "San Rafael Woman..." op. cit.

p. 50, "...canyon-like walls..." Boyd, Louise. *The Fiord Region...* op. cit.

p. 52, "Everyone who has gone..." Jones, Mary MacCracken. "Ice Woman Receives New Honor." *New York Sun.* June 12, 1939.

p. 54, "Here was a case..." Boyd, Louise. *The Fiord Region...* op. cit.

CHAPTER SIX

p. 56, "The real work..." "Woman Leader..." *London Daily Mail.* op. cit.

p. 57, "As being the only woman..." Lionel Askcroft. "San Rafael's Louise Boyd." *News Pointer.* San Rafael, CA, May 12, 1993, p. 12-18.

p. 62, "...fascinating and often beautiful..." Boyd, Louise Arner. *The Coast of Northeast Greenland, Special Publication no. 30.* American Geographical Society, 1948.

p. 64, "I'm reproached..." Jones, Mary MacCracken. op. cit.

p. 67, "Would the ice change?" Boyd, Louise Arner. *The Coast of Northeast Greenland.* op. cit.

CHAPTER SEVEN

p. 75, "Miss Boyd may claim..." Wright, John K., "Louise A. Boyd Arctic Expedition on the Steamship *Veslekari.*" *New York Times.* September 9, 1938.

CHAPTER EIGHT

p. 76, "I don't know..." "San Rafael Woman..." op. cit.

p. 77, "The dauntless leader..." "Woman Explorer Feted." *San Francisco News.* January 5, 1939.

p. 80, "No recognition..." "San Rafael Woman..." op. cit.

CHAPTER NINE

p. 84, "She's tall and slender..." "Woman to Explore Greenland." *New York Sun.* June 13, 1941.

p. 85, "But I always..." Gray, Nancy. *San Francisco Examiner.* June 1956.

p. 87, "I knew every inch..." "Woman to Explore..." *New York Sun.* op. cit.

CHAPTER TEN

p. 90, "which attracts everyone..." personal inteview with Marjorie Fountain.

p. 91, "L. A. B. [Louise Arner Boyd]..." ibid.

p. 92, "I'm just me." Miller, Hope Ridings. "Mrs. Henry Labrobe Roosevelt Gives Tea for Dr. Louise A. Boyd." *Washington Post.* May 26, 1939.

p. 93, "The captain told us..." Boyd, Louise Arner. Diary: *Flight Over the North Pole.*

p. 93, "North, north, north...." Boyd, Louise Arner. " A View from 9,000 feet." *Parade Magazine.* 1955.

CHAPTER ELEVEN

p. 95, "for conspicuous achievement..." Trott, Harlan. "Woman Honored for Polar Exploits." *Polar Times*. June 1959, p. 1.

p. 96, "enjoyed life..." personal interview with Marjorie Fountain.

p. 98, "I am kind of flabbergasted...." Gleason, Gene. "Geographic Society Elects Woman." *New York Herald Tribune*. February 8, 1960.

Index